Jewels In The Form Of A Bible

Words From The Author...

First and foremost I like to thank my entire supporting cast with help on putting this project together. I also would like to thank you the people, all the customers because I would have no success if I didn't have anybody to patronize. I also would like to thank my family and friends and the great promotion team that I had without actually putting one together. There is no set order in the way my thoughts came together to compose this project. There are different subjects addressed and without ubiquitous throughout the books entirely. My attention is to teach, motivate and grasp your attention. If you don't learn something maybe you can say a phrase out the book to someone else and they can learn something. If you go on to be successful and refer to my book or learn something you never knew or even use a cliché from time to time then I've left my mark and my mission is complete.

Richard Hall S.R

Giving is God's work.

Newsflash! We're all imperfect.

Knowledge is stronger than lifting weights.

A hater only remembers your pitfalls.

Understand what FORCE; is before you say someone hurt your feelings.

Having differences is part of being human.

Everybody you meet was a stranger at some in time.

Everything you want to ask somebody for, the answer is always no if you never try.

Just because you get a high off certain things doesn't mean you're untouchable.

Your family is who you consider your family, it's not always who is related to your mother and father.

For people who say they don't like being involved with dirty money, remember filling other people's children on your taxes is dirty money too.

Life goes by quick you don't get a new one. You learn how to write a sentence and if you're not careful you'll learn how to do one.

The ball doesn't bounce on your court when it's wet.

The wildest person out a crew usually isn't the richest.

Opinions are opinions but facts remain facts even if you don't agree with them.

Understand what comes along with being arrogant.

Don't blame your laziness on the white man.

Your children need to be taught more than what is learned in school.

A conscience is in your body from the time you are born.

There is not always an excuse an excuse for unfinished projects.

That was a lie when they told you words don't hurt because they can and it's also the reason you can be arrested for verbal abuse.

If you don't believe in yourself then how can you expect others to?

Some people are going to keep going back and forth to jail until they are too old to fight, run or hop fences.

All the devious things you do in life, remember you are not going to be young forever.

Most times when you bump your head it's because you are moving too fast.

For some people it takes a near death event for them to change their ways.

It'll take a diagnosis or an operation for some people to eat healthy or stop drugging.

Actual greenbacks have no value in this world.

Life experiences will teach you the same thing religious books do.

What good is talent that's not being used?

When you can recognize something about you is wrong, why not correct it?

Predictions really don't exist, it's really a good guess, even the weather man is wrong sometimes.

Is everybody that has a maid or a butler really that busy?
Or did the money just make them lazy?

Everybody that donates money gets a tax right off and gets
it right back, so is it all really from the heart?

Excluding drugs just about everything you eat and drink
has something in it that's good for your body except salt.

You can borrow money from the bank and they will charge you interest and that's legal, but if you borrow money from a friend and they charge you interest its loansharking.

A small baby that can't talk can be in a room playing with toys and its mother can walk in there and the baby may just look or utter baby talk. Take that same baby in the room playing in his mother's purse and the mother walk in there and the baby will jump! That's because right and wrong is in your body from the time of birth.

Just how you learn something you can forget it!

How can you expect to be good at something if you don't practice?

Books, the judicial system and punishments create fears and without them the world would be more chaotic than what it is.

How can you be in your twenties and possibly think you know it all?

God is not a he humans just need a way of communicating when mentioning him LOL!

In order to believe in God you have to believe in the devil.

Money isn't more important than people.

God, family, morals and standards should be the most powerful things on this earth but unfortunately its money and vagina.

There's always a time to be serious but life is supposed to be enjoyed.

Rumors don't define a person.

If you want to have something don't give anybody your last.

It's a difference between giving your last and giving your only.

Facts can be proven everything else is opinions and faith.

I can't do everything by myself that's why I pray.

The laws of nature don't change for one person.

Nobody is good in everything.

You got people that talk too much and you got those that let things speak for themselves.

Growth can take place when you can admit your weaknesses.

Sometimes your just wrong everything can't be justified.

Providing too much information to the opposite sex sometimes can be a turnoff and you may not even know it

Like a lot of tools the government uses, imminent domain is sometimes a form of bullying.

Why aren't jurors recorded during deliberations?

For financial people and investors, is anybody monitoring what the Basel group is holding back on government debt opposed to everyone else?

Are there any large banking firms that are 100% legit?

Banks don't have money they wait for you to give it to them.

Did you notice that when you bounce a check that you'll never get that actual check back?

A person who has conversations about coming out on top in everything he does must not be a human.

I wonder who put the formaldehyde in Osama Bin Laden's body and put him in the casket when he died LOL!

Ether is the drug in kilos of cocaine that's used to make them in the laboratory process. Ether is grown in the United States because South American countries are too hot to create it. Same as the coca plant it's grown in South American countries because the United States is too cold to grow it. Without ether there would be no powder cocaine. One grows in the U.S, one grows in South America. But Kilos are sent form South America to the United States with that good ol' U.S.A ether in it so how is there war on drugs?

I think I'm alive until I'm 80, the only thing that I don't like about saying that is turning 79!

When you hear things about people and you feel the need to repeat them make sure it's the good stuff.

I don't believe in man I believe in God.

There's no way to totally tell what a person has going on unless you have knowledge of all their business.

All of us are God of the earth; we are just not God of the universe.

It's not about who can be the most stubborn it's about who can be the most loving.

Break the silence.

Sometimes it's wise to listen to people that's older than you because they have been your age before and you have never been there's.

There's nothing wrong with employer taking advice from the employee.

Everybody has their time when something hits home.

There's nothing that can be created to stop death.

Sometimes when you're having too much fun too fast and mixing it with arrogance the same things will happen to you the opposite way!

Talking to your partner about your past can be a gift and a curse.

If everything went everybody's way we all would be professional gamblers!

Don't brag about bad things not happening to you, be grateful and thank God.

It's a bit insane to understand something about life and still go against it.

Good luck if you live your life worried about what everybody else thinks.

Always be a person of integrity.

Whatever role job or faction you choose in life, your goal should be at the apex.

Innovators are people who bring change to the world.

Yes it's true you can even be inspired by someone you don't like.

Don't be a sellout.

What you do and don't want to do doesn't always matter, God makes the decisions.

It's not always about being the smartest but use common sense.

A fact remains a fact whether you agree with it or not.

All books were written by humans.

When a black person is accused of murder they are called a menace to society, when it's a foreigner they are called a terrorist but when it's a white person they are called troubled or mentally ill.

The president or Government gets upset and send troops to kill thousands, but a normal citizen gets upset and kills one person and they give you life in prison, which quarrel is more legitimate in God's eyes?

A person is sentenced to death by lethal injection; those who inject the drugs are murderers too!

Prescription meds, alcohol, medical marijuana, tobacco, and firearms are all legal in stores. The only things illegal in this world is what the government doesn't make money off.

What's right, what's wrong? Who knows?

Knowledge is only useless if you are not using it.

It's not always about being a tough guy but sometimes you got to have guts.

You got to have mercy on people if you want God to have mercy on you.

Don't only call on God when you got a toothache.

To be elite is to excel in different fields more than the average person.

So the government has anti-trust laws! I wonder will they allow all their businesses and record books to go public so we "the people" can file the laws against them!

Women in congress are at a record high, does this mean they will finally be treated equally.

It's not that men cheat more, we just get caught more.

Men basically tell their best friends everything; women keep a secret away from theirs.

Men can't take everything they dish out to women, How many times have you heard about a married man or a man in a relationship getting another woman pregnant and his partner finds out about it and still stays with him and is even involved in the child's life and baby sits it? Quite a few right? Now how many times have you heard about a woman married or in a relationship and she gets pregnant by another man and her partner finds out about it and he still stays with her and is involved in the child's life and babysits? Very rare and almost second to none right?

Habits have power.

Fool me once shame on you, fool me twice shame on me!

A sucka' is born every day.

Some people will wash their chest in the morning if they couldn't see their face in the mirror.

We were all born for a reason, it doesn't mean that everybody will find their niche but we're all here for a reason.

There's no right or wrong age to get married people's situations are different.

I don't think it's a coincidence that homosexuals have the highest H.I.V rate, lesbians don't have the highest rate but homosexuals do, maybe something about that mixture creates it.

Physical appearance doesn't tell you about a person's qualities.

Read to succeed.

Don't do things that you don't want to do.

Be somebody!

Just a couple of words can mean a whole lot.

The outcome of one's existence starts with the way they're raised by their parent(s).

It takes a conglomerate of events and ups and downs to grasp an understanding of life!

What you see and sponge as a child helps shape the person you turn out to be.

No one man or woman will fully understand everything because we were created, we're not the creators.

Right and wrong is usually challenged by those who seek "Ill gotten gains."

Life is meant to be a beautiful thing, and it's molded by the choices and decisions one makes.

Whether good or bad all of us are bound and gagged by the flag of our country.

Life has religions, prisons, and other scares to maintain order because without them there would be chaos.

Life is beyond this earth and you can feel it like the connection you get when looking in a clear sky or being close to a body of water listening to its currents.

Life is nowhere near fair and some blame their predicaments on other people.

You got some people who base their life around the scare of a religious belief and because of that they rely on faith and do nothing to better their situations.

The mundane that are unemployed or even those who are content surviving check to check with basic jobs are what I call REGULARS!

Your complaints mean nothing if you're not taking action to make things better.

Trials and tribulations are a part of life regardless of your intentions or deeds. Everyone goes through stuff.

When evil or bad comes one's way he or she shouldn't say God is testing their faith for God doesn't test faith through evil as quoted in the book of James.

Karma is real along with weeping what you sow and those of normal intelligence know the consequences of their acts.

Time keeps going forward it doesn't matter if your clock or watch is broken.

It's your life and you're a fool if you let somebody else control it.

You can't control who you like or love but you know what's good or bad for you and you can control what situations you stay in. That's why there is such a thing as loving someone from a distance.

Those who live by their own rules and purposely go against the grain at one time or another are what I consider Gangsters.

The judicial system is the baddest gangsters I've ever seen.

Make plans, set goals and give your all into whatever you do if not you'll fail.

In order to believe in God you have to also believe in the devil because he exists and he's smarter than human beings.

God gives you free will to make your own choices. So he has his people and Satan has his also.

Get your tree of life in order which should be God, wife/husband, and kids. Mother and Father, family, friends, the needy and less fortunate.

With God first and family structure and right investments, your duties to your most high and purpose here should meet whether you have a religion or not as long as you believe.

Life is a never ending story.

Intelligent people write stuff down.

Second place is first losers.

A slap in the face doesn't have to be physically.

You'd be amazed what your brain can do if you use it.

You can get tired from mental exhaustion.

Don't take advantage of people, take advantage of opportunities.

Who cares about a broke legend?

What you had is worth nothing more than a conversation.

I can give you the tools it's up to you to use them.

Looking up to somebody is not determined by the height.

All seeds need natural positive things and without light you'll be very unhealthy and eventually die.

Children take in everything they see, you do, and everything they hear about you too.

The more somebody knows about you the more dangerous they can be to you, the more you know about them the more dangerous you can be to them.

School doesn't teach wisdom.

Yes babies are more angelic than adults and it's possible they see things we can't too.

Sometimes you are going to have to let some things go if you don't want to be tricked out of your freedom.

An egg fries under heat.

The only materialistic thing you can buy that doesn't lose value is a diamond.

Everybody is not financially stable. If you got something you want copywritten but you can't afford to pay for it, just mail it to yourself from yourself. It will come back to you stamped. It's called a poor Mavis copyright, and as long as you never open it, it'll hold up in a courtroom.

A woman's worst enemy is time.

You do certain stuff when you got the money and when you don't have the money there's certain stuff you're not supposed to do.

Rather you eat the ice or drink the water it doesn't matter if something is in it then, it's still bad for you.

Stop putting stuff off just do it!

More bad life comes out of the street life than good.

Being in the street is like sex, the safest way is not in at all!

Ambition.

Sometimes you got to take a few losses to have a lot of wins.

You can't be about business if you're always sitting down.

Sometimes sense ain't common.

As soon as you are ready to stop thinking, you are ready to die.

When you drink something real cold and it feels like you have brain freeze that's because of your trigeminal nerve.

Don't disadvantage yourself because of stubbornness.

It's more to life than just breathing, eating, sleeping, and using the bathroom.

Sometimes you got to pull the lever and pop the hood to let people know you are serious.

Don't spit on my cake and tell me its frosting.

If my aunt had balls she would be my uncle.

I swear some people can't lick a stamp!

Some guys have too much pride to say they want a bride.

A lot of people cut corners to get ahead, maybe that's why the world is round.

Wealthy people can't buy their way out of death.

Everybody needs somebody for something, even if you're a billionaire.

You can't pray and ask God to show you certain things and run away from them just because you don't agree with them.

Being a parent doesn't come with a manual or instruction book.

There are a lot of unwritten rules in the land of life.

Trying to be too power struck you might get hit by lightning.

If you can increase your finances without always increasing your lifestyle you'll have a whole lot more.

Business is based on performance and/or performance.

If there is an afterlife I wonder does that go for animals too.

It takes 23 chromosomes from the man and 23 chromosomes from the woman to make a baby. X and Y chromosomes, so I wonder how are clones made. Will they suffer in the afterlife if they live wicked?

Part of having longevity is having good temperaments.

If you take some money to the casino and exchange it for somebody's chips and cash it in that's a way of cleaning it.

Starting a corporation or an LLC is an entity. It's almost like your child becoming an adult and you are no longer responsible because if you take a loan out in your business name and you never totally pay it back and/or file bankruptcy and shut the business down that business will have bad credit and not you. It would be wise to write checks, pay some back and file your taxes properly to show where that government money went to.

Your glory days are not what declared you a strong person; it's what your overcome.

The strength of love doesn't always have something to do with how long you have been with a person.

Don't be the hammer that breaks the rock into pieces.

Successful people get up early in the morning.

Stay away from people that make penny wise decisions.

Recognize a person's worth when you are with them not when it is too late!

Some people should try getting along with their brain.

Be serious with some of the stuff you do. You really want to be a legend that bad?

Reverse the chemistry and do the opposite of what people expect you to do.

I'm never worried about what a female has done with somebody else I am only worried about what she is doing with me.

It's ghetto when a woman has wedlock sons by different fathers and both of them are all juniors.

The lower you set the cup the more dust falls in it.

If everything was just about you then you would be the only person in the earth.

Every gangster is somebody's hero.

Most of the time when you hear one side of the story it's usually in that person's favor.

No sin is greater than another in God's eyes but not in humans.

The softest dude that never told on anyone is realer than a gun totter whose name is on somebody's paperwork.

Sometimes when you are pompous things happen in your life that bring you back down to earth with everybody else.

When people say they oppose gangs it makes me wonder do they know exactly what a gang is.

Sometimes when you are not specific you can become confusing.

Everybody thinks the quote on quote bad guy doesn't have feelings.

Don't make purchases you cannot afford just to maintain your appearance.

You're not supposed to have one sided conversations with potential business partners.

Bill Gates isn't better than me it's about how you feel about yourself!

Being intimidated is obviously a form of fear, even if it's a pretty or dominating woman doing so to a man.

You know how when you are not on an important call people tell you to talk like you got some sense? Well if you just go ahead and educate yourself for real then you won't have to put up a front!

It's okay to get in position to hire people smarter than you.

It may be something rather unique or even weird about every legend.

We're all here for a reason, get your life together and leave your mark.

If you are a real family member or friend and you truly love somebody, whatever decisions or religion even if you oppose it as long as they're happy you should at least be happy for them.

There is a difference between a gangsta and a gangster.

Being a gangsta is more than just shooting, stabbing, and fighting. If you don't take care of your family then you don't fit the category.

College isn't what it used to be these days. Even if you have a degree you may still end up with a below average job.

A lot of people choose religion based on how they were raised as a kid. When you get older you should do your own homework and investigation and studying to support what you say you believe in. don't just blame it on when you were too young to make your own decisions.

Never show your hand, when a person hears something covert, clever or violent about you then they say they are surprised or that don't sound like you that's the way you want it.

Overall the government is the biggest gangsters in the world.

Life is not that bad. Sometimes you got to blow the worms out the way to drink the water.

If you want self-gratification that bad just stare in the mirror all day and cheer for yourself.

You can't keep flippin' the mattress, you are going to have to clean it in due time or get a new one.

You gotta understand that you are not always going to understand.

It's all about timing.

The body is the only thing that can't go where it wants, the mind is infinite.

Take care of what you sire.

The most important things to you should be priceless.

You can't always look at how old a person is sometimes you got to look at how old their soul is.

If a person raised chickens all their life with no other experience or exposure then how can you expect them to milk a cow?

If you live in a small city and rarely read or travel then chances is what you consider success or excelling very small.

When raising small children be careful of what you do and say. They are not always asleep at night. So either parent yourself or there is no sense in getting upset when your children mimic you!

Don't be confused by all these new technologies, with these apps, smartphones, webinars etc…don't be selfish it's all about I.

You don't have children just for them to room the house, go to school, surf the net and do things with their peers. They need guidance, that's why parents are called guardians.

You can't aid and assist a child's behaviors then in the same token tell them to do the right thing.

If you are looking for a person you like every single thing about, try a different planet.'

A job or somebody's rank or status doesn't give someone an invitation to be disrespectful.

Maybe if you looked at your cards from the bottom you wouldn't be so predictable.

There is nothing wrong with confidence sometimes it's okay to be cool!

There is nothing wrong with influence it's how it's used.

Guns aren't dangerous at all because they can't put themselves away safely and they can't use themselves.

Who cares how many weights you can lift if you can't think?

Even if you are consistently doing it, you are not going to be elite at everything but you'll at least be good or descent at it. Well newsflash it's the other way around when you are consistently doing something or not practicing it.

If you are in any type of entrepreneual retail business, confidence counts but you gotta show and prove because what matters is the patrons.

Don't wait until you get in trouble to do things you need to do to make your situation better.

Who moves first in chess doesn't matter, the one who moves lest is the winner.

Stop playing without me.

When a person has a fence up they don't want you to pass it without permission.

Whether it's a troop, soldier, or just an expression for love or a street life person, anytime a person wears a vest it's because they've hurt somebody, intend to hurt somebody, been hurt in the past, or think it's a high possibility of being hurt in the future.

Promising something and planning something are two different things so be careful what you hold people to.

Starting something on a file or writing it down has a better memory than your brain.

Sometimes to sell your product it helps to actually be a product.

Some people yearn for respect is fed though criminology.

What's more addicting drugs or behaviors?

The world is filled with more negatives than positives.

Some things put on the news and in newspapers are just to prevent a public outcry.

It would be nice but nobody is always right, sometimes you are left.

If you are infamous not famous that means you don't let everybody know what you are into by overexposing yourself by talking too much.

Humbleness can actually take you a long way and it doesn't mean you have to be gullible or a pusher.

Homework doesn't stop when you graduate from high school or college.

9 to 5'ers and entrepreneurs think different and raise their children different also.

George Mason is a black college predominately but the actual man is white and he was a part of creating the bill of rights, he also was for abolishing slavery that's the reason George Mason is a black college.

When the country goes in debt mostly because of their own complaciveness they raise taxes on the citizens as if it's our fault.

I wonder how the world leaders would take it if I could write what I really wanted to write as far as politics and the government! Would I be safe in this freedom of speech country?

Sometimes you got to reverse the chemistry. Put yourself in position and some of the people you reach out to may end up reaching out to you one day.

D.N.A stands for deoxyribonucleic acid and there is no way of avoiding it once yours is connected to anything or any child.

P.S means post script.

So when people get their name on a star in Hollywood I wonder what that means. Are they just recognition of someone's success?

When you learn how to be diverse you can relate or cater to all different kinds of people, races, and nationalities.

The way the internet has changed the world within ten years the only thriving brick and mortar retailers may be for consumable products and perishables.

Okay with all the tech savvy innovators am I the first one to predict smartphones partially being controlled by eyes?

20 years ago kids used to get sent outside to play a game and now they get sent in a room to play the game, and you wonder why obesity is up not only is adults but children as well.

The only love for physical music nowadays is shows and tours.

Don't let the internet and all these apps cause you to get bed sores!

Late birds don't get anything but dirt.

To some people the flaws in your life is remembered more than the good.

The Paine Webber Group is a covert name for the United States.

So they used Charley "Lucky" Luciano to help fight World War II. America consistently relies on a gangsta.

You have to be a talib before you can be a teacher.

Richer doesn't always mean smarter.

A crook can go straight.

Destined to be a legend.

Destined to be a philanthropist.

Destined to be political.

Destined to be unique.

Destined to be Elite.

Destined to be power.

Destined to be a thug.

Destined to be a gangsta.

Destined to be a ganster.

Destined to be broke.

Destined to be a loser.

People do different things for different types of acceptance.

Anything you do that doesn't come from the heart doesn't even matter.

Your intentions and your actions are really no different except when it comes to breaking the law.

How can you compare a human to material?

Isn't it weird to find a person that's arrogant but has no accolades?

If you base your relationships on what you got then a new person may never love you for who you are.

There is a certain way to conduct yourself when you become a role model especially when you know you're one.

Somebody is always watching.

The realities from the brain and life you can't Google.

Sometimes you got to do what everybody else isn't.

Don't just pray when it's bad, pray when it's good too.

Everybody has free will to do whatever they want to do but remember decision making can pay off to be a consequence.

Currents of water mixed with wind are stronger than a physical human.

Don't walk me around the mall of America to tell me something just get to the point!

Some things that are useful are very simple but why are you not doing it?

The first 8 presidents of the United States all served one year terms. George Washington was actually the 9th

president. The first president was a black man named John "swede" Hanson and he also created the first post office.

There are more ways to make money legally than it is illegally.

If you keep positive energy around you then positive things are bound to happen.

What do you really want out of life?

Don't be a waste of gravity.

Isn't getting paid under the table tax evasion?

Funds from barbershops and laundry mats can't be fully kept track of so do you think all of its owners report the rightful amounts to the IRS?

The world has nearly tripled over the past 50 plus years from 2.5 billion to 7 billion. Statistically every 13 seconds somebody dies but every 8 seconds somebody is born. So that's 3.2 people born for every 2 that die. So people have to die in numbers for population control. That's the reason for bombings, and some wars and all the diseases and sicknesses. They are not just happening out of nowhere or without prerequisites.

In man's eyes there is a sin greater than the other cause if it wasn't then there would be one sentence in a courtroom.

Sometimes it's going to be the next person's turn to come out on top.

Always have something to do.

A lot of wars are over money and bullying, commodities, natural resources and some are staged.

There is no such thing as catching cancer everybody is born with cancer cells in their body. The risk of them triggering is different depending on genetics, how well a person takes care of their body and sometimes it just happens.

So whatever happened to the weapons of mass destruction?

The only things that have value in the U.S.A are stocks, precious metals, property, and land.

Debit cards are assets credit cards are liabilities.

How come the host on donation commercials doesn't do them for free?

Take advantage of your life and cherish it because death isn't someone in a million surgeries, there's no chance of coming back.

You got a problem when you start talking about somebody else's business more than yours.

There just may be a cure for breast cancer, diabetes, arthritis, and other sicknesses, but since private companies have patents on a large number of genes in the human body, sometimes when a doctor comes along trying to study ailments to possibly find a cure he is hit with a royalty fee by owners of the genes so ultimately some of them just do away with the research. In reality that's like someone charging you to look at a star.

There is always something appealing to the eye just enough to get you to spend some money.

If you want to see things a little different and in some instances a bit clearer then start watching a lot of books and reading a lot of movies.

Don't test shallow waters and get mad when you drown.

The object of war is to win.

There are no rules in fighting.

So ironically Price Henry is a red head?

Don't lose out trying to always; make the biggest profit, a dollar is better than no dollar.

No matter what lifestyle you choose always have your heart in the right place.

There is a difference between a gangster and a psychopath.

Try getting into mind weights.

Never get into treating people any kind of way just because you can.

Throughout history most notorious leaders are highly intelligent.

Life is based on faith, death is the only truth.

If you are tired of living a destructive life, stop doing destructive things.

Stop making comments about how the next person has done all kinds of dirt and nothing major seems too happen to them, just get yourself in order.

Some elderly people that get sick and can't take care of them self or live out their last days in pain, it's not always just because they've gotten older, and it's because of the unconscious way they lived when they were younger.

You got people who'll make a bad decision and you got bad decision makers.

Nothing seems to go right for some people.

You can say the same thing without saying the same things.

The strength of your mind lasts longer than the strength of your body, and even if you stay healthy the strength of your body still will weaken.

Don't say sorry for things; apologize because a sorry person is no person.

The ring finger was chosen because it has a vein that runs directly to your heart.

Be careful what you say children don't understand.

The laws of nature don't change for one man.

Family shows it.

Sometimes you got to be like a carpenter; measure twice and cut once.

It's okay to be a perfectionist. Those that don't agree just don't have the same drive as you.

Whether you go to college or self-teach some type of higher learning is needed for success.

All originality should be patented.

When you abuse drugs they're in control.

You don't have to be going anywhere to keep yourself up.

The best possible exercise for the brain is actual exercise itself, but the second is the game of chess.

Voicemails are good because some messages are important but on another note it's a way for people to say what they want to say without you cutting them off or saying anything back.

Music can be a form of medicine, a depressant, upper, or downer sedative.

Be careful what you write and say anti-gay rights are powerful these days.

How could you think it is okay for your cars, jewelry and clothes to be richer than you?

Mentally ill people don't know any better, crazy people do!

An adult acting out is worse than a child doing it.

Like humans primates, dolphins, and whales all have neuron cells. They're not as smart as humans but that explains their intelligence.

Technically everybody is older than their age at least 2 months to every year. In the B.C times we used to be up under the 10 month Roman calendar. The months July and august derive from the emperor Julius Caesar and his nephew Augustus. These months were squeezed in because September stands for 7 and October 8 and December 10. If you think about it anything that got something to do with OCT such as octagon stands for the number 8. Anything that got something to do with DEC like a decagon or a decimal stands for the number 10. That's because October was the 8th month and December was the 10th.

You don't always get in trouble for hanging with the wrong people, sometimes you're the wrong person!

If you want to keep track of important mail just send it under return receipt request. Meaning somebody will have to sign it, and the receipt will be mailed back to you.

So insider trading is illegal but say I'm wealthy and you're wealthy and we're friends. We both have IPO's and we're both invested in each other's company. You don't think I'm going to tell you if mine is about to plummet and vice versa?

Not a single Jew showed up to work the day of 9/11 bombing. With that much power I think of it as Jewunited States Of America.

When the Columbian government was after Pablo Escobar they wouldn't let his family leave the country. When the U.S government was after Osama Bin Laden George W. Bush flew his family out the country.

Fluoride used to be used as a poison to fight with in war and now it's used as something on your teeth.

Google is only going to have the answers to what the government allows. Of course that doesn't include their secrets.

I like drones because they help us in war plus if one of them is shot down we don't have to worry about losing troops.

Cubans are finally getting a little freedom. Who is better in power Fidel or Ravi Castro?

Business is shrewd, that's just the way it is.

The senate and house of reps controls the FBI's budget that's why some of their wrong doing whether its bribes or inside trading will lend to get overlooked instead of their budget being inconvenienced.

People tend to still ball up when they're resting because that's how you were in your mother's stomach.

Women usually lotion their entire body down. When and if s man does use lotion normally it's mainly only on his torso.

It's a lot more credible when you show a person what your words mean.

Kids are the only ones who should be indulging in social networking fights.

A tax I.D number is just like a social security number. In fact your social security number is your tax I.D. until you get one if needed. If you apply for one in your name that's a new set of numbers that you may even be able to use in case of background checks for job apps, cars, signings, leases or other business. After all it's in your name and it's yours so it should trace back to you. Not guaranteed but it might.

Don't ever fall out of the habit of watching your own money.

You don't have to own a house to get insurance. You can get renter's insurance too that way you're protected if your home is ever burglarized.

If you don't eat pork and you buy a slice of cheese and pepperoni pizza and pick the pepperonis off what's the difference?

Carbon 14vdating dates back up to 50,000 years old on trees, rocks, clothes, and fossils. Not once were there human bones discovered and someone was abnormal age like anywhere between 200 to 800 years old.

They say everything man made can be duplicated huh? Yeah except the pyramids of Gaza.

Everything is not going to sound logical like hot ice and fried ice cream.

You don't have to have a religion to believe in God.

You don't wake a sucka' up.

Remember the element of surprise! Don't prepare anybody for something that doesn't work in their favor.

Your time will come you just got to recognize it and seize the moment(s).

Jewels in the form of a bible is exactly what the name says. This book isn't vulgar but it's not for children and in some instances it may be a little too deep for adolescents. I touch different walks of life, wear many hats and shoes and act as a cosmopolitan. This book is a relative to the streets, politicians, entrepreneurs, regular working people, up and comers, the wealthy, rich, middle class and poverty stricken. The messages given in this book come in different ways. Some humorous and some very serious. There are religious quotes, some subjects about God and also some breakdowns about understanding what's gangster and understanding what's stupid. You picked the right book if you're looking for some quotes to use as motivation especially if you yearn to be prosperous. I also delve into the tricky ways that politics work and some covers that are pulled over U.S citizen's eyes. I predict that some of my quotes will be used in everyday life and even become teaching tools. I always felt that what I know or creatively put together through wisdom and intellect wasn't meant to be kept to myself. My selfless nature gains satisfaction from those who are touched by any subject or quote out of my book enjoy.

RICHARD HALL

S.R

www.ingramcontent.com/pod-product-compliance
Lightning Source LLC
Chambersburg PA
CBHW081458040426
42446CB00016B/3290